CHAIRS,  Chairs, CHAIRS!

by

Cynthia Cappetta

Illustrated by

Rick Stromoski

Rookie reader®

Children's Press®
A Division of Grolier Publishing
New York • London • Hong Kong • Sydney
Danbury, Connecticut

For John, Kate, Dan, and Sarah
—C. C.

For Molly
—R. S.

Reading Consultant
Linda Cornwell
Learning Resource Consultant
Indiana Department of Education

Visit Children's Press® on the Internet at:
http://publishing.grolier.com

Library of Congress Cataloging-in-Publication Data
Cappetta, Cynthia.
Chairs, chairs, chairs! / by Cynthia Cappetta ; illustrated by Rick Stromoski.
p. cm. — (A Rookie reader)
Summary: Presents, in brief text and illustrations,
different kinds of chairs and their uses.
ISBN 0-516-21542-6 (lib. bdg.)   0-516-26474-5 (pbk.)
1. Chairs—Juvenile literature. [1. Chairs.] I. Stromoski, Rick, ill. II. Title.
III. Series.
TS886.5.C45C37   1999
645'.4—dc21
98-9916
CIP
AC

Some chairs are soft.

Some chairs are hard.

Some chairs stay inside.

Some stay in the yard.

Some chairs are high.

Some chairs are low.

Some chairs carry people
over the snow.

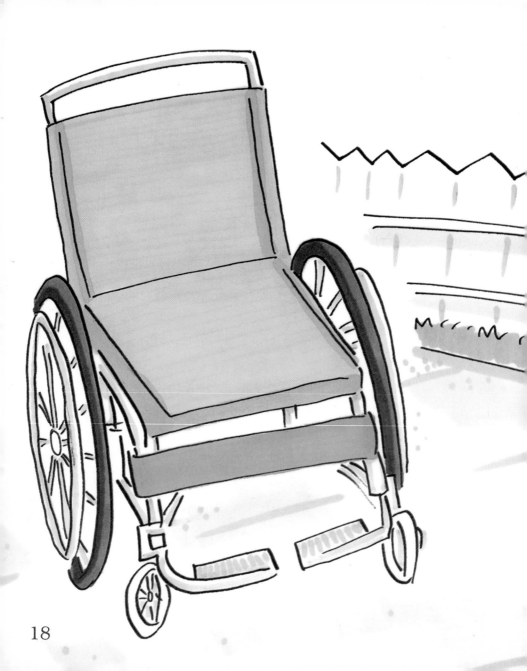

Some chairs with wheels . . .

. . . help people go.

Some chairs go up
and then come down.

Some chairs
let people twirl around.

Some chairs are for work.

Some are for rest.

What kind of chair
do you like best?

WORD LIST (39 WORDS)

and	for	low	then
are	go	of	twirl
around	hard	over	up
best	help	people	what
carry	high	rest	wheels
chair	in	snow	with
chairs	inside	soft	work
come	kind	some	yard
do	let	stay	you
down	like	the	

ABOUT THE AUTHOR

Cynthia Cappetta lives in Middletown, Connecticut, with her husband and three children. She has taught at various levels and currently enjoys working with toddlers and their parents. She has lots of chairs in her home.

ABOUT THE ILLUSTRATOR

Rick Stromoski's award-winning cartoons and illustrations appear in national magazines, newspapers, and children's books. He lives in the historic district of Suffield, Connecticut, with his wife Danna and daughter Molly.